2 Minute MOTIVATION

HOW TO INSPIRE SUPERIOR PERFORMANCE

Robert W. Wendover

Sourcebooks
Inc.

Naperville, IL

Published by: **Sourcebooks Trade**
A Division of Sourcebooks, Inc.
P.O. Box 372, Naperville, Illinois, 60566
(708) 961-3900
FAX: 708-961-2168

Editorial: John Santucci
Cover Design: Wayne Johnson/Dominique Raccah
Interior Design and Production: Wayne Johnson, Sourcebooks, Inc.

This publication is designed to provide accurate and authoritative information in regard to the subject matter covered. It is sold with the
understanding that the publisher is not engaged in rendering legal,
accounting, or other professional service. If legal advice or other expert
assistance is required, the services of a competent professional person
should be sought.

From a Declaration of Principles Jointly Adopted by a Committee of the
American Bar Association and a Committee of Publishers and Associations

Library of Congress Cataloging-in-Publication Data

Wendover, Robert W.
   2 minute motivation : how to inspire superior performance /
Robert W. Wendover
         p.   cm.
   Includes index.
   ISBN 1-57071-019-8 : $14.95.
   1. Employee motivation.   I. Title.   II. Title: Two minute
motivation
HF5549.5.M63W449   1994
658.3'14—dc20   94-29647
                                                     CIP

Hardcover—10 9 8 7 6 5 4 3 2 1
Printed and bound in the United States of America.

Read what they're saying about...

2 Minute Motivation:
How to Inspire Superior Performance

"Congratulations! You have done it again. *2 Minute Motivation* cuts through the latest fad theories and presents its concepts in an efficient and simplified manner. Managers will want to read this book again and again."

Frank A. Smaola, President
Merlin's Muffler and Brake

"*2 Minute Motivation* is an easy-to-follow, common-sense approach to inspiring employees. Why can't all management be this easy to understand?"

Jeanne Larson, Manager
Regional Marketing / Customer Service
NIKE

"This book is great! *2 Minute Motivation* puts into words what it takes years to develop and implement."

Jackie Meyers, Manager
Human Resources
The Gates Rubber Company

"*2 Minute Motivation* is a thought-provoking read which pleasantly consumed an 850-mile plane ride. You've successfully mapped out an easily-applied process to stimulate employees through improved communications. Your principles are sound and worth employing. I'll be sure to share it with my peers."

Timothy M. Richards, Manager
Sales Development
General Electric Company

"Congratulations on a great book. With change in the workplace accelerating, motivation is of paramount importance. *2 Minute Motivation* is right on target."

Robert W. Gras, Vice President/CFO
International and Business Development Group
US West

"Good things come in small packages, only this time they are in a wonderful little book called *2 Minute Motivation*. Thanks, Bob! I can appreciate the concise writing about a topic we all need to work on continuously."

Lee Perino, Director
Human Resources
Western Farm Bureau Management Corporation

"*2 Minute Motivation* is common-sense management for a common-sense world."

Gail Forsyth, Manager
"Your Idea / Your Universe" Suggestion Program
AT & T Universal Card Services Corporation

"With the labor force changing the way it is, *2 Minute Motivation* will put you several steps ahead of the pack when it comes to motivating employees."

Allan Sterbin, Director
Human Resources Selection and Evaluation
The Promus Companies
(Hampton Inns, Embassy Suites, Homewood Inns)

Dedication

To you who strive valiantly for innovative ways to motivate those in the workplace: may this book be a source of inspiration for years to come.

2 Minute Motivation

Table of Contents

2 Minute Motivation

Introduction

Motivation. Productivity. Self-esteem. The success of any organization rests on these three concepts. But why are some managers better at this skill than others? What does it take to motivate those you lead?

Understanding what lies behind the actions people take and the things they believe is essential to inspiring them. *2 Minute Motivation* will enable you to better determine what motivates your employees.

If you are a new manager, you'll learn how to turn your theories about motivation into practical application. If you have supervised people before, this book will help you gain even deeper insight into how to inspire each individual and turn them into top performers. You'll discover what they require from you as a leader.

You will begin to see what has been holding your employees back from giving you complete loyalty and effort. With the specific strategies in this book, you'll discover how to regain your employees' trust, commitment, and dedication to their jobs.

The principles you will learn will help you avoid getting in your people's way, which could limit their growth and defeat their sense of accomplishment. Instead, you'll discover what they need in you as a leader, and you'll know exactly how to provide these things for them.

To influence an employee's attitudes and behaviors, a good manager arouses interest and enthusiasm. Meeting people at their own level of interest is the key to developing an effective relationship.

It is tempting to measure motivation based on our own experience and standards. While you know what you believe, it may be very different from what triggers those around you. Whether communicating with an employee, friend, colleague, or even a spouse, you may often be left wondering why they don't respond to your positive messages and actions. While they may understand your intentions, you may fail to reach them where it counts: at their level of interest.

2 Minute Motivation is a guide that will enhance your understanding of those around you. It provides a step-by-step recipe for the actions you must take to improve your leadership skills with your employees.

No person excels in relationships without the help and support of others. What you do with what you observe, along with how you act, determines your own success. It is simple to say that you must observe and respond to the behavior of others. As a process, that is all it takes, but polishing your observational skills and refining your actions is what this book is about.

In an age of frantic schedules and hurried decisions, it is easy to overlook the obvious keys to inspiring the performance of others. All too often, managers take their employees' existence for granted and fail to give them the individualized attention they deserve.

Yet, by dedicating yourself to being a better observer and to being more committed to treating others as unique individuals, you will make great strides in inspiring your people to exceed your own expectations of them.

This is not just a business book; this is also a "people book." These principles apply at home, on the playing field, in your place of worship, and in all your personal and professional associations.

2 Minute Motivation is not simply a two-minute activity. It is a series of two-minute opportunities which will help you better understand others—their biases and behaviors—and will give you specific strategies for dealing with them effectively. You'll learn how to arouse better productivity and increased morale by applying these principles.

Read this book and reframe your approach to motivating those with whom you work every day. Grasp the concepts and discover abundant new ways for inspiring outstanding performance.

The Secrets of
2 Minute Motivation

Chapter 1

Motivating people is not a complicated, time-consuming process. It does, however, require keen observational skills and the ability to organize the information you gather about others. Every person's motivation is a result of his or her experiences, perceptions, and attitudes.

If you manage or supervise others, you know how difficult it is to find the right keys to motivation. Inspiring others to do a good job may seem to elude you a great deal of the time. Remember...

You cannot force other people to be motivated, but you can provide the stimulus for them to motivate themselves.

If you want to encourage coworkers to improve the quality of their work, for instance, you must first understand how they perceive the work they do. Each individual reveals his or her attitudes by using "self-talk."

What is self-talk? It's the voice you use to talk to yourself as you go through your day. Whether you are aware of it or not, you are constantly asking yourself questions, expressing your opinions, or giving yourself warnings. What you say to yourself is a result of the information you already have stored about a great number of subjects.

If you are trying to decide between two products, for example, your self-talk might be saying, "The red one's really nice, but the blue one goes better with my car...." This internal voice helps you decide which product to choose based on what preferences and opinions you already have about the colors, red and blue.

At other times, your self-talk may reveal questions you have about a problem or issue. As you read this, your self-talk might be saying, "What is he talking about?"

In response, you might say to yourself, "I don't talk to myself, do I?" and realize that you are doing it right now! We can never get away from this continuous process we use to talk to ourselves.

Everybody uses self-talk: your friends, coworkers, boss, and spouse. These little conversations help reveal the attitudes you have about every topic and every person you encounter.

So, in order to motivate your employees, you must first examine their attitudes, or what they are saying to themselves. If an employee is making assumptions based on incorrect or insufficient information, then his or her attitudes may lead him or her to jump to incorrect conclusions or to take the wrong actions.

★ ★ ★

Employees who are unmotivated often base their attitudes and actions on incorrect or incomplete information. In order to motivate them, you must give these employees enough correct information to change their self-talk into something more positive. This will in turn help your employees to make more reasonable decisions.

If you want to motivate an unenthusiastic office worker for instance, you must understand what that person is saying to themselves. On one hand, the employee may be saying, "This job is so boring, I'm going to go out of my mind!" On the other hand, they may be saying, "I haven't the faintest idea what I'm doing. Maybe if I do as little as possible, I won't get into trouble."

Obviously, the employee's self-talk is very different in each of these instances. It is crucial that you discover what employees are saying to themselves. That way you can determine how to motivate this individual. In one case, the worker may need more challenges; in the other, additional job skills may be necessary.

The only way to find out which of these two scenarios is true in this employee's case is to observe, ask, and listen. Very few employees will take the initiative to approach their boss and say, "I'm bored" or "I'm in over my head."

The comments an employee makes in the office, during meetings, or to others over lunch can provide valuable keys to the nature of his or her self-talk. How he or she acts, the decisions he or she makes, and the quality of work can also help you understand what's going on inside his or her head.

If you take these observations and add them to the information you already know about this worker (such as work history, education, and level of confidence), you will develop a detailed picture of how you can best motivate him or her. You'll be able to encourage your employees' productivity and satisfaction on the job.

*You can't motivate
other people...*

*But you can provide the
stimulus for them to
motivate themselves!*

Gathering these insights does not happen overnight. You gain more understanding over time. The observations you make and the bits of information you discover about your employees come as a result of talking and listening to them in two- or three-minute opportunities, from time to time.

During these chances to interact, you have the opportunity to coach, encourage, or challenge them to do a better job. Hence the title of this book: *2 Minute Motivation.*

2 Minute Motivation can help you reframe the way you motivate others. Using two-minute opportunities will prove so effective that soon they will become habits you incorporate into your daily management style. You don't have the time to sit down with each employee for an hour to figure out what makes them tick. You must accomplish this through observing and interacting with your employees repeatedly, but for just minutes at a time.

You can apply the principles in this book in the frantic pace of today's world. The amount of work you must accomplish each day often requires you to react quickly to the situations you face. If you don't take charge of the way you motivate your employees, you will lose your opportunity to steer them to greater productivity and higher self-esteem.

It's easy to assume that every leader wants to get better at motivating his or her employees. But following through on those desires to improve your skills is a different matter.

It is easy to become distracted by other priorities and place your employees' need for guidance on a back burner. Without consistency, however, keeping people inspired becomes an impossible task.

People tend to think of themselves first. Because of this, many supervisors make the mistake of assuming that others think and feel the same way. This could mean a supervisor may falsely believe that the things which motivate he or she as a supervisor are the same things that motivate his or her employees. If a supervisor forces his or her likes and dislikes on these other people, the effort to motivate them will fail.

★ ★ ★

Never assume your people

see a situation

the same way you see it!

★ ★ ★

Listen with passion to what your employees talk about. What inspires you may completely turn off someone else. Your love of sports, for instance, may discourage another person from wanting to interact with you because they perceive you as a "jock." Just the same, you may believe that those who bury themselves in books or academic study are boring. To be a good motivator, you must develop the ability to keep your values separate from those of your coworkers. When you do, you will be well on your way to finding the best ways to motivate others.

Above all, you must be consistent and sincere when trying to motivate others. The way you communicate with employees reveals your own internal beliefs. If others suspect you are being insincere to them, not only will you fail to motivate them, but in fact you will discourage them.

Your employees care about how you treat them. They also notice how you treat others. If you show favoritism or dislike to anyone, these behaviors will discourage employees from trusting you.

Being consistent in the way you react to each person means treating everyone fairly. You must be consistent in the amount of time you talk and listen to each person, in the way you reward and discipline, and in your overall management style in order to demonstrate your desire to be fair.

Using two-minute opportunities to inspire your employees demonstrates your trust, consistency, caring, and understanding. People who believe they are trusted, cared for, and understood will not only meet, but exceed your expectations.

People have a way of rising or falling to meet other people's expectations of them. Your ability to instill the desire in your employees to satisfy your high expectations will help determine your success in getting outstanding performance.

Building a productive team is impossible unless you recognize the differences in how each person is motivated. You are leading a diverse group of people. Your ability to build a team out of those individuals depends on your skill in recognizing each team member's individuality.

Motivating others means constantly recognizing and acknowledging what your employees are contributing to the cause. If you are inconsistent in the way you motivate your people, they will respond with a lack of effort and diminished productivity.

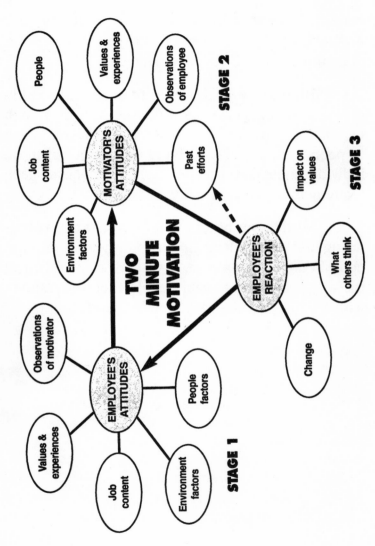

Understanding *2 Minute Motivation*

The *2 Minute Motivational Process* consists of three stages. A diagram of the process is on page 16.

The first stage is to consider the individual's actions and attitudes as they are revealed to you in the workplace. These actions and attitudes help you determine the person's values, level of self-esteem, understanding of their job, past experience, and how they respond to both the work environment and to others in the organization.

The second stage is to consider how your actions and attitudes influence your ability to motivate other people. Your actions and attitudes are based on values, experience, self-esteem, and understanding of your job. You are also influenced by your observations of the individual, the work environment, other people in the organization, and the results of your past efforts to motivate that person.

The third stage is that person's reaction to your attempts to motivate him or her. How he or she reacts depends on the person's ability to cope with change, what he or she believes other people will think, and how well your action meets his or her needs and corresponds to his or her values.

After your employee reacts, you must make a mental note of how he or she responded so you can later evaluate how effective you were in motivating him or her. (Refer to the dotted line in the diagram.)

The key to using **2 Minute Motivation** is to stick to the two-minute format. These short time intervals provide repeated opportunities to better understand your employees and to steer them in a positive direction. A couple of examples might help:

Example No. 1: You overhear someone discussing the difficulty they are having learning a new set of product codes. While you don't want to interrupt the conversation, you take note of what is being said, for future reference.

In this example, the second step is to spend a short amount of time talking and listening to your employee and trying to understand what you can do to meet her needs. You might engage her in a conversation about product codes at the coffee stand for instance. During that discussion, you may teach her a quick game that you used to play to help you remember the codes and their meanings.

The third step is to assess your employee's reaction to your attempt to motivate her. In this example, she will consider how comfortable she will feel with your suggestion. She might consider what others will think of her when she is playing the game, or she may wonder whether the game makes sense to her.

At this stage, you will want to note your employee's change, or lack of change, in behavior. She may play the game and learn the codes, and her motivation may go up. If she resists the game, her motivation will either remain the same or decrease. In either case, you, as the motivator, must make a mental note of your employee's response for future reference.

Example No. 2: The work of a long time employee has been slipping over the past two months. He has also become more arrogant in the way he responds to coworkers. While no one has said anything to you, you can detect a level of tension whenever this person is in the work area.

The first step is to examine the values, attitudes, and background of this person. He has been an employee longer than anyone else in the department. In fact, you learned a great deal from him when you took the position, even though you were the manager.

He has been through the automation that took place five years ago, not to mention the hassle with the new telephone system that almost put the company under. He has probably trained half the people in your department because you didn't have the time.

In truth, everyone in the department should be thankful this person is around. Yet about two months ago, he proposed a new system at the staff meeting that was immediately shot down by everyone else. There was nothing wrong with the plan. In fact, it would improve overall customer service. But it was obvious that it would mean additional work, and no one was in favor of that.

Ever since that meeting, this person has been arrogant and, sometimes, downright caustic with other employees. Lately, this person has been prefacing everything they say with, "You weren't around then, but the way we used to do it was..." Maybe that's a signal that he felt put down by the newer employees.

The second step is to examine your own motives and feelings in relation to this person. How you feel about him is going to have an impact on how you try to motivate him.

When you first began supervising him, you were a little intimidated since he knew the systems and you didn't. But after a few uncomfortable encounters, you finally resolved your feelings and he has supported you ever since.

You respect and admire his contribution to the department. Yet when he came up with a good idea, you let the other employees defeat it without giving the idea a good hearing. He probably felt abandoned in the meeting. After the meeting, he may have decided to stop making suggestions if they were going to fall on deaf ears. Now it's up to you to find a way to re-motivate this person and encourage his contribution. But you want to do it discreetly.

The third step in *2 Minute Motivation* is to develop and implement ways to motivate the person. You might begin by bringing up his original idea in conversation by saying: "What ever happened to that idea you had a couple of months ago about servicing customers? I kind of liked it." Wait for his reaction. If it is hostile, ("You ought to know. You let it get shot down in a meeting.") then you'll need to try a different approach. If he seems open to the idea of discussing it, look for ways to build support for it in the department.

You might bring it up at a staff meeting and give this person a lot of credit. If other employees try to shoot it down, go to bat for it. Ask why they are so against it. Do they have a better solution? Even if the idea is not implemented, this person will see that you are supporting them.

Find other ways to recognize this person. Encourage him to contribute and work to ease the tension between him and other employees. If his work continues to slip, then you will need to discuss it. But this can be done without the confrontation the earlier situation may have caused.

Throughout this process, make notes on what worked to motivate him and what didn't. Chances are you'll need to motivate him again.

The Three Keys to 2 Minute Motivation

The first key to inspiring outstanding performance is to know your own values. Your values influence everything you do and think. How effective you are with anyone or any group depends on how well you understand what influences you.

Motivation is not just a top-down process. Everything you experience with others is filtered through the screen of your own experiences and biases. Exploring your own values is critical to understanding the values and motivations of others.

The second key to inspiring outstanding performance is to recognize diversity in people. It's very tempting to stereotype people in many ways. We tend to take a broad-brush approach and conclude that all those with a particular similarity respond the same way.

While deep down we may know that stereotypes are far too general in nature, it is easier to assume these generalizations than to make the effort to pay closer attention to the character of each individual separately.

Using a broad-brush approach works against us by sending the message that we do not care for individual differences. Your ability to individually tailor your actions to each person with whom you come in contact is a key to inspiring him or her.

Each person is a unique combination of experiences and heredity. Even identical twins vary significantly in their actions and attitudes. Those who are able to ferret out these differences will be rewarded with trust, caring, and understanding.

The third key is to recognize the value of these individual diversities. What can you do to help those you work with take advantage of the diverse strengths of others in the workplace?

A person of Native American heritage, for instance, might be the best person to deal with a difficult customer of a similar background or heritage.

In another situation, you may find that a veteran may be the best choice to approach military accounts. The fact that he or she understands the "military way of thinking" puts the customer's mind at ease and helps them to find common points of communication.

While you must be careful of stereotypes and myths, recognizing a coworker's strength in dealing with a particular situation demonstrates that you value that worker as a person, rather than just another employee.

Simply celebrating an employee's personal accomplishment outside of the workplace shows your concern for their well-being. The value of recognition goes a long way toward building long-term motivation in every individual.

Individual diversity includes many things. To understand these differences, begin by making a list of your employees' physical characteristics. You will include traits such as age, height, physical appearance, weight, attire, skin and hair color. Continue by writing down their skill levels in various job-related activities, their formal education, and the training they have received since they began the job that they now have.

Consider each person's work, social and military experience, family background, nationality, economic situation, and sexual orientation. These, among other factors, combine to form a complex picture of each person with whom you work and interact.

But before you explore the things that influence other people, take a look at yourself. How do you think other people see you? Understanding the way you affect other people is a vital link in motivating them.

If you don't know how your employees perceive you, ask them. However, make sure you do so in a way that encourages honest feedback. Your employees must know that you will not penalize them for whatever information they tell you.

Motivation begins with understanding the individual, but it extends beyond this point. Other factors must be taken into consideration. Consider your environment. Think about the policies, schedules, pace, physical layout, and other characteristics which color it. How do these things work together to inspire outstanding performance? How do they hinder performance?

Consider the corporate attitude at your company. By simply walking through a work environment, most people can get a clear feeling of the general attitude of the people who work there. How do people get along with each other? Is there an atmosphere of caring and cooperation, or one-up-manship? Does the group, as a whole, desire success?

Finally, consider how the people in general respond to change. Is change mostly positive or negative? Trying to motivate someone who is afraid of change requires a different approach than someone who welcomes change and sees it as more of an opportunity.

The same holds true with a group. You must be prepared to address the group's apprehensions. How has change taken place in the past? How do they respond to different types of changes?

Successful change can be very motivating. Unsuccessful change can be debilitating. You must pave the way for making changes positive by listening to your people's comments and concerns and taking them into account. Motivation cannot be forced. Even if you feel a person needs to be motivated, he or she may not necessarily agree. By observing them, you can determine his or her attitude toward change and motivation.

In summary, tailoring what you do to meet your people's needs is the key ingredient in finding the best way to motivate them. Each person has his or her own set of values, ideals, and emotions. Simply insisting that he or she accept your values, ideals, and emotions will result in unmotivated employees.

2 Minute Motivation will help you inspire those around you to outstanding performance and greater job satisfaction. For the most part, good leaders are aware of the principles we have identified. What are you doing to stimulate enthusiasm, commitment and high self-esteem in the people you deal with daily?

As you use the two-minute concept we have discussed in this chapter, you will be able to respond to each person in your organization as a unique individual. And, most importantly, remember the three stages of motivation:

1. Consider your employees' attitudes before you try to motivate them.

2. Think about your own attitudes and behavior and try to keep them from negatively influencing your attempt to motivate employees.

3. Evaluate how your employees react to your attempts to motivate them. Keep this information in mind to use the next time you interact with each individual.

In the next four chapters, you will learn specific ways in which you can use these simple techniques to inspire outstanding performance in those you manage.

The *2 Minute Motivator* remembers that:

1. The keys to *2 Minute Motivation* are: observation and action.

2. You cannot motivate people. You can only provide the stimulus for people to motivate themselves.

3. To understand how a person thinks, you must tap into his or her self-talk.

4. Unmotivated people are basing their actions on incorrect or incomplete information.

5. To motivate someone, you must anticipate his or her attitude and behaviors.

6. Motivation must be consistent and tailored to every staff member.

7. People will rise or fall to meet your expectations.

Inspired employees

are happier employees.

Uncovering Employees' Hidden Motivations

Chapter 2

Where do people's attitudes and values come from? How do their beliefs affect their sense of motivation?

Every individual has a different set of experiences. That person's perceptions of the workplace are based on those experiences. In trying to motivate them, it is your job to discover which variables impact each person within your organization and how these variables affect their behavior.

The information you gather about each person will provide you with valuable insight into what motivates them at work. This information includes personal elements such as the person's age, education, and work experience. But it also includes less subjective elements such as what the job is, the nature of the work environment and the personalities of coworkers.

No one wants to psychoanalyze those who report to them. But as a supervisor, you must filter your attempts to motivate them through the observations you have made of that person's performance and attitudes. While the elements just mentioned are constantly present, different ones affect the person's decisions and emotions at different times.

A staff member may respond positively to you most of the time, yet may become obstinate when a particular coworker is in the room. This lack of cooperation might be tied directly to some bad feelings about that coworker. Having observed this reaction, you might make a mental note not to attempt to motivate this person when that coworker is in the room.

In another situation, you might notice that a staff member leaves the room whenever one or more smokers enter it. Based on this insight, you may be able to improve this person's productivity by providing a smoke-free work area. If, on the other hand, you decide to eliminate smoking from the workplace, consider what impact that will have on the smokers' motivation.

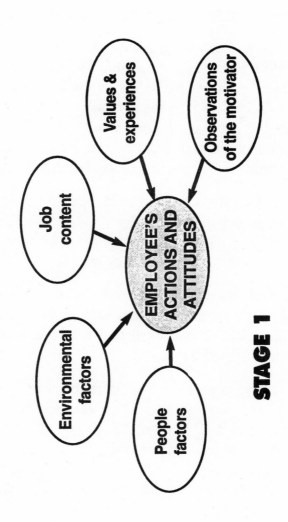

Factors Affecting Worker Motivation

As you can see from the diagram on page 35, there are a host of elements that impact how a person reacts on the job. Some might be considered internal factors such as the person's values and background. Others may be considered external such as the work environment and job content. Each of these factors influences the motivation of each employee.

Let's take a look at each one and how they impact the people you manage:

External factors

Job content: What the job is all about is central to how people view their existence within the organization. Therefore, it is critical that they feel comfortable doing the job every day.

Many people who fail in their position do so because they have difficulty developing the skills and understanding of what the job actually requires. This feeling of inadequacy leads to feelings of frustration and lowered productivity. If the situation is not resolved, it can lead to anger and eventually termination or resignation.

For example, if a retail clerk seems to be making an unreasonable number of mistakes, it may mean she is having difficulty understanding the new computerized cash registers. You may have thoroughly trained her on the new system, but a little encouragement and review may be just what this person needs. While this advice may sound like common sense, do you follow it as often as you can?

A critical part of any motivator's job is to determine how well each person on their staff understands the job.

Work environment: While being able to adequately define their job is critical, a healthy, stimulating work environment is also important. A person's work includes everything in his or her physical surroundings such as lighting, the color of the paint on the walls, the number and location of windows, and the size of each individual's work area.

It also includes the general work pace, noise level, and neatness (or sloppiness) of the working environment. There are also more subtle factors which influence people's perceptions of their place of work. Among other things, this includes the reliability of the copier and other office machines, availability of supplies, and how easily someone can figure out the telephone system.

All of these factors, plus many more, combine to create an atmosphere that affects different people in different ways. While some people might adjust well to a messy work area, for instance, it might send others into a frenzy.

Overall frustrations such as an unreliable copy machine can be a real drag on morale. ("I wish they would just fix the blessed thing!")

People factors: Every person who works for an organization impacts everyone else. Those who survive best are the people who can adjust to and accept a variety of coworkers.

As you progress through each day, keep an eye out for actions and comments that give you clues about how people interact with each other. Who gets along with whom? Which people are pals? Which personalities are more outgoing? Who keeps more to themselves? And which employees are natural leaders among those you supervise?

In addition to noting what's generally going on in these personal relationships, consider the factors already mentioned such as the pace of activity, noise and stress level. By taking a step back to see the big picture, you'll have much better information for directing your motivational efforts.

For instance, one of your employees may prefer a quiet setting in which to concentrate. Another may thrive in a more lively environment where people yell ideas back and forth. Taking the time to discover which employees prefer what particular working environment will help you find the most effective ways to motivate them.

Each of these external factors impacts your employee's overall desire to contribute and share in the workplace. These elements also contribute to their self-talk (what people are saying to themselves while they work).

Internal factors

In addition to the external elements which influence motivation, people are also affected by internal elements. These include their personal values, level of education, degree of self-esteem, and their feelings toward you, their supervisor.

These internal factors have a significant impact on your employees' self-concepts. Their self-concept, in turn, has a bearing on their level of motivation. As you know, a person's mood and their self-concept vary from day-to-day and even hour-to-hour.

It is your job as a motivator, to observe each person's actions and comments in order to detect how they might best be motivated at a given time.

Values and Background:

A person's values and background can be divided into three categories, each of which contain several components:

> Experience
> Heritage
> Physical factors

Experience includes the following:

Work: What jobs has this person held? In what industries? How well did he do in these positions? What successes or failures has he had? How long did he stay in his previous positions? Why did he leave? What are his career goals? How long has he been in his current position?

Education: What formal education has the person had? High school? Trade school? College? Graduate school? Any specialities?

Marital status: Is the person married? Divorced? What is her spouse like? What does her spouse do? Do she appear to have a healthy relationship?

Parental status: Does the employee have children? How many? How old? What are the children like?

Income: What is the employee's salary history? How much does he make now? Do these wages seem fair for the person's job level? How do the wages compare to those of his peers? Does he appear to live within his means? If not, how much does he seem to spend? Does this person have financial concerns?

Military experience: Is the person a veteran? What branch? Where was he stationed and what did he do? What rank did he attain? Which years did he serve? Does the employee have any issues or concerns about their past military experience?

Hobbies and sports activities: What hobbies do your coworkers enjoy? How enthusiastic are they about them? How often do they talk about their personal

interests? Are these interests related to their job?
Are their hobbies used as a healthy or unhealthy way
to escape?

The second category which influences a person's values and background is *heritage*. This category includes some sensitive issues. Therefore, it is
wise to be careful when asking questions so that others are not offended. These may include the
employee's religious and political beliefs, along with
their racial background.

Be very careful, however, when gathering this
information, that you do not to misuse it. While
knowing as much as possible about your people can
help you lead them better, they must be treated as
distinct individuals. Stereotypes must be avoided at
all costs.

Avoid stereotyping

at all costs!

Heritage includes:

Religious beliefs: Does your employee attend a place of worship? Which one? How involved is she? Does she feel comfortable sharing her beliefs? Do co-workers accept this?

Political beliefs: What are the person's political beliefs? How strong are they? Is he affiliated with a particular party? Does he regularly talk about them? How do coworkers respond to the person's political preferences?

Race: What race is this individual (Black, White, Hispanic, Asian, etc.)? Does she exhibit any stereotypical attitudes or behaviors that may correspond to her ethnic background? Take a good look at your own stereotypes to see if they are valid. How is she viewed by coworkers?

Ethnicity: What is this person's nationality? How does he relate to his heritage? Does he feel comfortable discussing it? How do you know?

Sexual orientation: Is this person male or female? Does he or she seem comfortable talking about gender-related issues, or are such topics to be avoided? How does he or she generally feel about both men and women?

Geographic location: Where did this person grow up? Does he carry any conscious stereotypes about the region he is from? How proud is he of his geographical roots?

The third category influencing a person's values and background are *physical factors* that include:

Age: How old is this person? How does her age compare with the rest of the employees? Are there general stereotypes about age that you see being expressed by this person? Are there others in the organization who have particular attitudes about age? Are there mandatory retirement policies?

Physical and mental abilities: Is this person able-bodied? If not, what kind of limitations does he experience? Is he sensitive about any of his physical attributes (weight, appearance, height, etc.)?

These values and background factors can play a critical role in helping you discover what motivates the individuals you lead.

Observations about you, their supervisor: The final factor you must consider about your employees' attitudes is how they feel about you, their supervisor.

Like it or not, you are a role model for everyone else in the organization. Your actions and comments are analyzed by every member of your team and they influence how your people feel about their jobs.

You will probably find those who disagree with your point of view harder to motivate because they will be looking for flaws in you, your actions, and your decisions. On the other hand, those who see most things your way will generally strive to support you.

Your ability to determine how each person you manage feels about you will help you conclude which motivational strategies will work for each of them. While motivation is still a series of trials and errors, predicting your employees' behavior in advance will give you an advantage in inspiring them.

For each individual, all the factors we've mentioned combine to form their level of self-esteem on the job. This self-esteem varies from day to day, depending on circumstances related and unrelated to the workplace. It is essential that you learn to adjust your behavior to your employees' varying moods and personal concerns.

An employee might be feeling very good about his or her job for instance, but a disagreement with a spouse may hinder him or her from doing his or her best that day at work. Your skill at detecting these changes in mood and finding ways to get your employee back on track will help determine the overall productivity and level of self-esteem of your workers.

An essential key to using *2 Minute Motivation* is being able to grasp the opportunity to ask questions that will help you identify each individual's values and desires.

Having a two-minute conversation with two employees about a particular project, for instance, may help you discover that one person particularly enjoys creative tasks, and another prefers detail work. Knowing this about each of them enables you to carefully tailor their projects in the future, thereby producing better productivity and motivation in each.

If you are in touch with a person's values, you can anticipate their responses, actions, and emotions. In other words, get to know your coworkers! Being pro-active in motivating them is a critical element in inspiring superior performance.

Motivation is not something that is turned on and off as we get to work. These principles hold true in more than just business settings. They can also be applied at home, in volunteer organizations, professional associations, and in your place of worship.

Opera singer Beverly Sills once observed that the best part about her job was that she got to do it rather than that she had to do it. Your ability as a leader, to inspire others to look forward to doing their job, is an essential element to maintaining and enhancing performance at all levels.

Pages 50–60 contain a selection of questions you should be asking about your employees. Remember that it is better to gather this information in an informal manner through observation. In asking employees directly, you may not obtain totally honest answers.

The *2 Minute Motivator* remembers that:

1. Every person has a different set of experiences, values, and attitudes.

2. Any attempt to motivate someone must be filtered through what you know about him or her.

3. The elements which affect a person's motivation include external factors, such as the other people in the working environment.

4. They also include internal factors such as the person's level of self-esteem.

5. How you, the supervisor, are viewed by your staff affects your ability to motivate them.

6. An essential key to motivation is to grasp two-minute opportunities for asking questions and discovering more about each individual.

Employee's Understanding of Job Content

✓ Does this person understand how his or her job fits into the organization?

✓ Does he or she have the skills required to complete the job successfully?

✓ Does he or she clearly understand your expectations of job performance?

✓ Does he or she know specifically how he or she will be evaluated?

✓ Does he or she understand where additional help and resources can be found?

✓ Does he or she know how his or her performance can both meet your expectations and exceed them?

✓ Does he or she feel adequately trained to perform the job?

Employee's Observations of the Supervisor

✓ Does your employee believe you have an "open door" policy?

✓ Does he or she consider you approachable?

✓ How frequently does he or she formally evaluate your performance as supervisor?

✓ How does he or she feel his or her comments about you are acknowledged?

✓ Does he or she believe you are a team leader?

✓ Does he or she have experience working with you in a project setting?

✓ How does he or she perceive your social skills?

✓ What words would this person use to describe you as a person?

✓ How would he or she describe his or her own level of trust in you as a supervisor?

✓ How would he or she describe you as a role model within the organization?

✓ How would he or she evaluate your approach to rewarding positive behaviors? (Does he or she believe your approach is consistent?)

✓ How would he or she describe your overall style of supervision?

Employee's Values and Experience

✓ How would you go about determining your employee's values and ethics?

✓ What comments and actions has he or she made that are clues to his or her values?

✓ How would you describe his or her work ethic?

✓ How would you describe his or her level of integrity?

✓ Where did your employee work in the past?

✓ What attitudes did he or she experience in those settings?

✓ What responsibilities did he or she have?

✓ Why did your employee accept his or her present position?

✓ What education and training has he or she had?

✓ How closely matched are the duties in his or her present position with his or her training and education?

✓ Does he or she appear to be internally or externally motivated?

✓ How much does he or she rely on you for motivation/inspiration?

✓ How much does he or she rely on coworkers for motivation/inspiration?

✓ What particular areas of interest does he or she have on the job? Off the job?

✓ How does he or she perceive his or her present job fitting into the rest of his or her life?

✓ How does he or she help or hinder coworkers in the completion of their jobs?

✓ In what terms would you describe his or her level of investment in the job?

✓ In what ways does he or she exert additional effort where needed?

Environmental Factors Affecting the Employee

✓ Which factors in the work setting make your employee's job easier or harder to do?

✓ Are the proper resources available to help him or her to accomplish the job?

✓ How controlled does the employee feel in the work environment?

✓ How does the pace of work help or hinder your employee's ability to accomplish the job? (Volume of tasks, complexity of tasks, rate of change in tasks, and responsibilities)

✓ What is the balance between quality and quantity of work?

✓ Does the organization provide a physically comfortable environment? (Ample work space, comfortable furniture, adequate lighting, suitable level of noise, easy-to-use telephone system, etc.)

✓ What factors in the work setting help or hinder communication between employees and between the organization and its customers?

✓ What factors in the work setting encourage or discourage your employee's trust?

✓ What are the signs of segregation between supervisors and non-supervisory employees? How do these factors help or hinder performance?

✓ How do you segregate yourself from those you supervise? How do each of these factors help or hinder your employee's performance?

People Factors Influencing the Employee

✓ How is a strong work ethic perceived by your employee?

✓ What influence do other employees have on this employee?

✓ In what terms would you describe the level of trust among employees?

✓ What influence does this level of trust have on this employee?

✓ Under what circumstances does this employee "follow the crowd"?

✓ Under what circumstances does this person "avoid the crowd"?

✓ How likely is this person to participate in "group think"? And under what circumstances?

Exploring Your Values and Motivations

Chapter 3

We spent the last chapter examining the elements which influence your staff's motivation. Now it is time to explore your own. What motivates you?

Your values and attitudes about how to inspire others depend on how you feel about yourself. While every staff member needs your leadership, how you motivate each one depends on how you feel about:

➠ That person
➠ Yourself
➠ Your job
➠ The organization

You may tend to pay special attention to the people whom you consider "rising stars." But as a supervisor, you must learn how to feel comfortable in your position to do so. On the other hand, if you perceive "rising stars" as threats, you might have second thoughts about encouraging them. In both cases, it is wise to look at your own feelings toward various staff members.

In another instance, you might try motivating an employee by talking about promotions because you value promotions. If the employee is more interested in spending more time with his or her family, however, your strategy will fall on deaf ears.

Being in touch with the values that influence you and your behavior is critical to inspiring others. Keeping this in mind, as well as remembering the elements that influence your staff members, paints a clear picture of how you can spark others to perform as you wish they would.

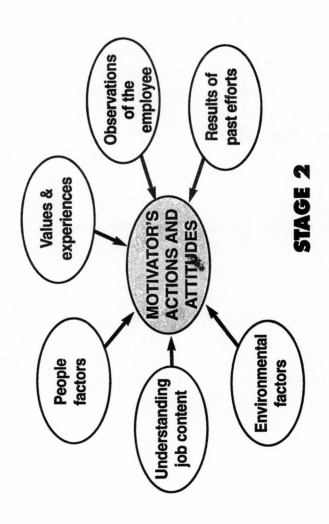

Factors Affecting Your Motivation

As you can see from the diagram on page 61, your motivation is influenced by the same motivational elements as those you supervise. When the information and insights from these factors are combined, they create your attitudes and emotions about your job, organization, and those with whom you work.

If you like your job, you will naturally want to encourage and inspire others. When you dislike your job, or have job-related problems, your mood will reflect this through your actions, comments, and overall demeanor.

In spite of how you feel about your job from day-to-day, it is essential that you provide inspiration for those you supervise. Your ability to recognize how your values, background, and emotions influence others will enable you to find the most effective ways to motivate them.

Exploring Your Motivational Biases

As you approach every opportunity to influence your people, a variety of thoughts will pass through your mind. Just as the people whom you are supervising use self-talk, you also use it.

What does your self-talk say when you are trying to inspire another person? It might begin with a review of events such as, "Sandy seems to be stuck in a rut. She used to come up with so many suggestions. The past couple of weeks she's gotten awfully quiet."

Then your self-talk might wander to, "I remember when my employee, Ralph, blew up at that customer service problem last year. He'd been awfully quiet right before that. I wonder if there is something brewing with Sandy like there was with Ralph when he was so quiet."

And finally, it might suggest a strategy like, "Sandy has to meet with me tomorrow regarding the new uniforms. I think I'll poke around a little then. That way, she won't feel like she's being confronted without warning."

Throughout this internal discussion you're having with yourself, another internal conversation may bring up issues related to you. This part of your underlying self-talk might say, "I get so tired of having to keep my eye on other people. Every time I turn around, somebody is having some kind of problem."

To a thought about about how Sandy might be ready to blow up, your self-talk might respond, "I don't want what Ralph did last year to happen again. That made me look really stupid!"

Finally, your self-talk might leave you with, "On the other hand, if I can get Sally really fired up again, it'll make me look real good. I wouldn't mind that pat on the back."

All through this secondary conversation, there is one common theme: W.I.I.F.M. (What's In It For Me?). This is a natural response. Most people are in the habit of thinking about themselves first. There is really nothing wrong with that—some even call it a survival instinct. But people must balance their self-interest with consideration of others.

Being pro-active in

motivating others is a

critical element in

inspiring superior

performance.

You cannot motivate someone without first being motivated yourself. Just as your staff needs to feel comfortable in their jobs, you need to feel comfortable in yours. Your job as a supervisor is often more complex than that of your employees. But you share the same emotions and mental challenges as your employees.

If you feel frustrated about the way things are going, your mood and patience will fluctuate. If things are going well, you're apt to be more generous, happy, and understanding of others.

As mentioned, the diagram on page 61 describes the elements involved with your own motivation and your ability to motivate others. Once again, they are divided into external and internal factors.

External Factors

Just as each of your employees is influenced by internal and external factors, you are too. While you may view these factors from a different perspective, these elements contribute to your sense of confidence and self-esteem.

Your understanding of your employee's job content: Not only does each employee need to understand exactly what their jobs require, you must have a clear understanding as well.

Chances are, you are supervising at least one person whose job duties you have not performed. It is essential then that you know as much about that person's day-to-day activities as possible. Not only does this ease tension when this person is absent, but, more importantly, it gives you a perspective on what they are going through. By understanding this, you will be better able to develop strategies to motivate this employee.

Even if you held this employee's position in the past, chances are the day-to-day responsibilities have changed significantly. Ask questions to find out which job elements are the same, which are different, and which are particularly challenging to the employee this time.

She might, for instance, have to deal with a computerized version of what you used to do manually. For this reason, she may have more detail to cope with. Working to gain a new perspective on the employee's job also demonstrates that you care about her and what she does all day.

Work environment: For the most part, you, as a supervisor, are affected by the same environmental factors as others in your organization. A broken toilet, or lack of paper for the copier, not only frustrates you as the person in charge, but it frustrates others, too.

The major difference between you and those you supervise is that you have the power to alter your environment (or at least a portion of it). While you may not be able to have windows installed in a windowless office, you may be able to have the walls repainted from dingy gray to bright yellow or white.

You also have the authority to change day-to-day routines that prove to be inefficient or cause tension among your staff. Eliminating unnecessary procedures, for instance, can do much to motivate your entire staff (not to mention affecting the bottom line).

When you think about how to best motivate others, reflect on how the surrounding environment affects all of you. Do what you can to improve the working conditions and procedures that influence everyone in your organization.

People environment: Not only does the physical environment affect others, but the people environment also has an effect. If staff members insist on working individually instead of as a team, there may be problems you need to investigate. These interpersonal problems can have serious effects on people's attitudes and morale.

Just as you can influence the work environment, you, as supervisor, can take steps to encourage healthy ways for people to interact with each other. The approach you take in trying to foster good relations among employees should be tied to the needs of the individuals in your organization. The more you are in touch with their desires and needs, the more you will be able to predict how they will react to the things you do.

Detecting discontentment over a particular policy and addressing that issue may not in itself improve motivation. But the fact that you were willing to discuss your staff's feelings about it may help them reduce their negative reaction to the policy.

As you attempt to motivate your people, remember that they may have the same concerns about working relationships as you do. Put yourself in their place and imagine what emotions they might have about the other people in the organization. Taking time to recognize these concerns with them will demonstrate that you are in touch with those in the workplace. That fact in itself will help stimulate goodwill.

Results of past efforts to motivate: It is natural to expect that every person on your staff will need to be motivated from time to time. Sometimes you will succeed in your efforts; other times you may not.

For instance, you may have used a particular method to encourage an employee to improve her customer service skills. She responded positively for one week, and then fell back into the same pattern she used before. In another situation, you noted that this same person made a complete change in her behavior and continued to demonstrate this change.

Why did she respond to one approach and not the other? What was different about the two attempts? Did you reason with her differently in one instance versus the other? Was she in a different mood during one instance?

While we cannot always predict why people do what they do, we can look back at their track record or general pattern of behavior. Make a note of what approach works with each member of your organization. Compare this information with other things you know about them.

You may have discovered, for instance, that whenever your assistant starts to talk about cycling, he goes on forever. When you suggested that he organize a company cycling club, he did not get excited, but he did get fired up about competing in a citywide cycling contest.

In examining the differences between these two related ideas more closely, you may discover that he thrives on competition but detests organization. Perhaps this is the reason for his less-than-acceptable work at maintaining reports. What can you do now that you have made this discovery?

By using these techniques, you will be better able to predict how best to motivate each person on your staff.

Being in touch with

your own motivation

is essential to

inspiring others.

Internal Factors

Values and background: As is true with every person you supervise, your own values and experiences influence the actions you take. Some of your experiences add to your skills as a supervisor, while others may detract from them.

You may learn over time, for instance, that listening is a much more effective supervisory skill than talking. At the same time, these same experiences may have made you impatient with "inane coworkers who can't get anything right the first four times!"

While this example may be an exaggeration, it demonstrates how each experience can be interpreted in a number of ways. Your ability to apply the best of these lessons will help make you a more effective motivator.

The factors we have covered while trying to better understand those you supervise are the same ones you must take into consideration for yourself. Gaining perspective on how these same elements affect you in your working relationships will provide the insight you need to locate the most effective motivational triggers.

By using these techniques, you will be able to predict how best to motivate each person on your staff.

Your formal education, for instance, may have stopped after two years of college. Yet you are supervising people who, in some cases, have attained master's degrees in their fields.

While day-to-day conversations may not reflect it, you might feel intimidated by their level of education. Perhaps you even feel frustrated that you never finished your degree.

Yet you may also have five years of management experience while your coworkers have just entered the workforce. Being able to keep feelings about your formal education in focus is essential to your ability to think clearly about how to motivate these individuals. For all you know, they may be concerned about their lack of management experience and are looking to you for inspiration.

In another instance, you may be of Hispanic heritage. The primary language spoken while you were growing up might have been Spanish. As a result, it is possible that you are self-conscious about your accent.

While you are an experienced manager who was promoted on your merit, there might be someone in your department who feels favoritism played a role. How do you find ways to motivate someone with this attitude? (You might begin by determining whether the person in question actually feels this way?)

In a third situation, you might be twenty-four years old while those you supervise are as much as thirty years your senior. You know you are fully capable of doing your job, but you get the feeling that others may not take you seriously.

What can you do to motivate coworkers old enough to be your father? Upon investigating, you might discover that some are happy to have a supervisor with some youth and energy in the department. Or you might discover that for some, simply asking their advice and counsel will inspire them because of their feeling of a need to contribute.

Examining your values and experiences as they relate to those you supervise will always provide some insights for finding new inspiration.

Observing Employees

It is your job as supervisor to observe people's actions every day. But to effectively motivate each individual, you must look a level deeper— deeper than just looking at their behavior.

One person may be able to maintain an acceptable performance, and yet hate his or her job. Another might appear to be having the best time in the world, but is not meeting even your most minimal expectations. While you are not expected to be a mind reader, each person's non-verbal communication will reveal most of what you need to know.

Consider the people you presently supervise. Which ones have consistently been your best performers? What have they done which makes you feel that way? Is it that they meet your expectations, or that they take the initiative? Do they always seem to "save the day?" And what have you done to encourage them?

Now consider those who are not meeting your expectations. What traits, if any, do they all have in common? What are they doing (or not doing) which makes them poor performers? How have you tried to motivate each one of them?

The big question in motivation is "why?" Why are some people motivated while others are not? Why do motivational strategies work with some people but not with others?

The more you know about each individual with whom you work, the better you will be able to answer these questions. Here are a few tips to observe each day:

Keep an eye on body language. The vast majority of what we communicate is done nonverbally. This includes facial expressions, eye contact, posture, hand motions, level of enthusiasm, the way someone walks, etc.

Listen to more than just what the person says. How is it being said? In what tone of voice? How much is he or she participating in conversations and meetings? How confident is his or her voice?

Examine this person's track record. What topics really generate excitement or interest? Which topics does he or she avoid? Are there issues which cause anger? How does he or she interact with others?

Test your assumptions. If your employee appears upset, ask her about it. She may say, "No!" But then you know for sure. Or if someone seems depressed or frustrated, investigate the situation. Drawing conclusions without having the facts can prove to be one of the biggest de-motivators of all.

Understanding what motivates you and how you feel about your own job and the people you supervise is essential to helping you develop a consistent style of inspiration for others. Your ability to anticipate and respond to their needs demonstrates how much you care for each individual you supervise.

Consult pages 83–92 for a more complete list of questions to ask yourself about your values and motivations.

The *2 Minute Motivator* remembers that:

1. Attitudes about motivating others depend on how you feel about yourself.

2. Every time you try to motivate someone, your behavior is influenced by your own biases.

3. You need to make an effort to clearly understand the scope of each of your employees' jobs.

4. When trying to motivate someone, think back about which methods have worked in the past.

5. Personal values will influence your perception of others.

6. Making assumptions is usually counterproductive when motivating others.

7. Looking deeper than a person's behavior helps you to discover what is motivating that person.

Motivator's Values and Experiences

✓ How well-matched are your job responsibilities with your formal education and training?

✓ How well-matched is your previous work experience with your present job duties?

✓ How well do your values and work ethic fit into your job?

✓ How much do you rely on others for motivation/inspiration?

✓ Describe your level of interest in supervising and motivating others in relation to the other duties in your job.

✓ How does your job fit into your life balance? (eg. work to live vs. live to work?)

✓ Why did you accept your position?

✓ What are your aspirations for your position?

✓ What motivates you to do a better job?

✓ What factors in your job make you feel uncomfortable?

✓ How does your level of comfort in supervising your employees influence your ability to motivate them?

Motivator's Observations of the Employee

✓ Does your employee complete work on time?

✓ Does he produce quality work?

✓ Does she provide input and suggestions for improvement?

✓ Does he volunteer for extra projects?

✓ Does she initiate work?

✓ How much training/instruction does he generally require?

✓ How much coaching does she generally require? What kind of coaching?

✓ How does he demonstrate his level of trust in you as a supervisor?

✓ How does she show her enthusiasm for her job?

✓ How does he demonstrate his cooperation in working with others?

✓ What projects and/or tasks gets her excited?

✓ How does he demonstrate that he feels motivated?

✓ Describe your level of comfort in motivating this employee.

Environmental Factors Influencing the Motivator

✓ What factors in the work setting make your job easier or harder to do?

✓ Are the proper resources available for you to accomplish your job?

* How controlled do you feel by the environment?

✓ How does the pace of work help or hinder you in accomplishing your job? (Volume of tasks, complexity of tasks, rate of change in tasks and responsibilities, etc.)

✓ What is the balance between quality and quantity of work in your job?

✓ Does the organization provide a physically comfortable environment? (Ample work space, comfortable furniture, adequate lighting, suitable level of noise, easy-to-use telephone system, etc.)

✓ What factors in the work setting help or hinder communication between employees and between the organization and its customers?

✓ What factors in the work setting encourage or discourage employee trust?

✓ What are the signs of segregation between supervisors and non-supervisory employees? How do these factors help or hinder your performance?

✓ How do you segregate yourself from those you supervise? How do each of these factors help or hinder your performance?

People Factors Influencing the Motivator

✓ What influences do your employees' attitudes have on your actions?

✓ What factors within the organization's bureaucracy influence your decisions?

✓ How do you perceive yourself in comparison to other supervisors?

✓ How do other supervisors perceive you?

✓ How does your boss perceive you?

Results of Past Efforts to Motivate the Employee

✓ How do you define motivational reward (your opportunities to acknowledge and encourage positive behaviors in your employees)?

✓ How have you rewarded this employee in the past?

✓ What techniques have worked? Why?

✓ What techniques have not worked? Why?

✓ How do you tailor motivational rewards to this employee?

✓ How do you elicit his or her input about motivational rewards?

✓ How do you know when you have been effective?

✓ What do you do to encourage this employee's motivation?

✓ Does what you do help promote this employee?

✓ How do you determine an effective reward structure for him or her?

Motivator's Understanding of the Employee's Job Content

✓ Have you served in this employee's position?

✓ Describe your understanding of his or her job duties and how he or she fits into the overall organizational structure.

✓ Describe your understanding of performance expectations for this employee's job.

✓ In what terms would you describe this position's influence on the organization?

✓ In what terms would you describe the organization's influence on this position?

Inspiring Motivation in Others

Chapter 4

Inspiring motivation in others is both an opportunity and a risk. If you succeed in motivating an individual, you will also arouse that individual's increased interest and productivity. If you fail to motivate that person, you run the risk of losing your effectiveness as a supervisor.

Motivating others contains three major elements:

➡ The attitudes and values of the person you are trying to motivate.

➡ Your own attitudes and values.

➡ The person's reaction to your attempts to motivate him or her.

We have already covered these first two elements in chapters two and three, but now it's time to explore the third: the person's reaction to your attempts to motivate him or her.

As you examine what motivates you and others, a variety of ideas will come to your mind about how to approach different situations. Every individual you work with will present a different series of challenges to your ability to motivate that individual.

Some of your top performers, for example, might tire of routine work very quickly. Your major challenge with them is to provide new stimulation.

Your marginal performers will probably require more one-on-one attention in order to help maintain their focus and attention to detail.

Your consistent performers, or those who make up the backbone of the organization, will probably require your regular support and encouragement.

Each person within the organization is, above all, an individual, even though he or she may fit into one of these three categories. Once you are tuned into his or her values and sense of self-motivation, you will need to find consistent means of encouragement.

The three or four individuals who form the backbone of your staff are each motivated in different ways. While they all will most likely respond to attempts at team-building, each has certain needs which, when met, will trigger his or her internal sense of inspiration.

One employee may be extremely devoted to his family. Therefore, asking about his family, or perhaps sharing about your family, may encourage his sense of belonging and self-esteem.

Another employee might be an avid football fan. Asking her about who's going to win the Super Bowl on the opening day of training camps may show her you care about her as a person.

A third employee may be pursuing a business degree at night. By periodically sharing how you juggle your management and budgeting responsibilities, you may inspire this person to work even harder. (In this case, lending support and understanding during exam time will also go a long way to building goodwill.)

As you attempt to motivate each person on your staff, three elements require your consideration. As you can see from the diagram on page 97, every person is evaluating your attempts to motivate him or her from several different angles.

This evaluation once again comes in the form of self-talk. This means that the mental voice provides facts, biases, background, and predictions, or a sort of "play-by-play" analysis of what could happen. The three elements you must consider are:

➡ The person's orientation toward change.
➡ The person's perception of what other people will think or say.
➡ How this attempt at motivation impacts this person's values.

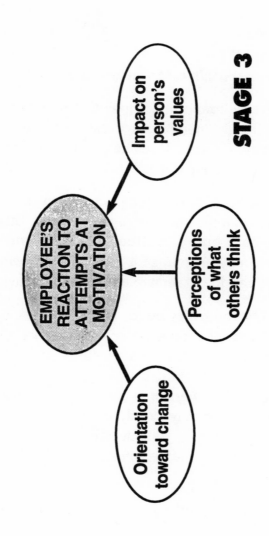

The person's orientation toward change.

How comfortable does this person feel with change? Is the person set in his or her ways, or is this person flexible? Does he or she look forward to new ways of doing things?

Some of your attempts to motivate may not require a significant change of behavior. Buying an employee a cup of coffee or talking sports, for instance, may encourage a sense of well-being. And these things do not require a change in behavior.

On the other hand, you may seek out this person's thoughts on a better way to process orders. If he or she is open to change, he or she will probably jump at the chance to exert some influence. However, if this person is comfortable in his or her "rut," he or she may simply provide some marginal input just to satisfy your questions. And unless you pursue the issue, the person will probably forget that it ever came up.

Understanding a person's orientation to

change before you make an attempt to motivate them is a key predictor to your success. This leads us to your second consideration:

The person's perception of what other people will think or say.

Most of the way your workers evaluate this element comes through their self-talk, which is based on their experiences both inside and outside of the workplace.

You may, for example, begin delegating additional tasks to a particular person because you know she enjoys doing them. While she may be appreciative of your efforts, she might also be concerned about what her coworkers will think. Her self-talk might go something like this:

"Rob's really making an attempt to follow through on his promises to delegate new responsibilities to me. What he's given me will provide some great experience.

"But what will my coworkers think? I saw how they razzed Betty when she got that promotion. Am I in for the same treatment? After all, I party with these people after work! I know it is in my best interests to take on new tasks, but maybe I'm not ready for all this."

As you can see, even your best intentions toward helping an employee can be thwarted by his or her assumptions and fears. By taking the time to anticipate an employee's apprehensions, you, as supervisor, can work to help the employee overcome them.

You might say, "I know you enjoy being one of the gang out there. I also know that you have a real desire to learn this part of the job. How do you think we should approach this?"

By asking for the employee's feedback, you are demonstrating your concern about her place in the group. At the same time, you can gain additional insight about what motivates her.

Some people are more concerned about appearances than others. It is your responsibility as a motivator to take these issues into consideration. The third element you must consider is:

How this attempt at motivation impacts this person's values.

Values play a large role in determining whether a person will respond to your motivational

By asking for

employee feedback,

you are demonstrating

your concern about

their place in the group.

attempts. When factors such as a person's conscience, emotions, and sense of fairness come into play, they may sometimes override the person's resistance to change or concern about what others may think.

A marginal worker, for example, may respond to your suggestions about getting more work done, because deep down he knows he is hindering productivity. He may be a very loyal worker who is stuck in a rut. He may also be the party organizer in the department.

Yet if you anticipate these concerns, you may be able to build a motivational rapport that will enhance this worker's productivity and keep him productive. You might begin by asking about the next party coming up. Does he have enough help in organizing it? Can you help in any way?

From there, you might mention your "concern" about his slipping productivity and how it is having an impact on everyone.

He will probably say something like, "Yeah, I know. Sometimes I get a little distracted. I've been doing this for so long, there's nothing challenging about it."

You might respond, "I've watched you do great work in the past. What can we do to make your job more interesting?"

At this point, his self-talk may be, "She's right—I have been marking time. But I'm comfortable where I am and there are all these great people around. What would they think if I suddenly started being a high-producing, straight-arrow kind of guy?"

"On the other hand, maybe that's what they're waiting for. I really haven't been pulling my weight. I need to get my act in gear."

From here, you will probably see a substantial improvement in this person's productivity. But motivation does not stop here. If he comes up with suggestions for making his job more interesting, act on them. If he starts to slip, remind him of how much everyone is counting on his participation. And don't forget to compliment him on his party-organizing skills.

Once your attempt to motivate an employee takes place, two events occur. First, the employee records your attempt to motivate, and his or her own response. The employee will use this information again when responding to your future attempts at motivation. This information, pleasant or unpleasant, becomes part of the person's values and background and is critical to his or her sense of motivation.

Second, you are also recording the person's reaction to your attempt so you may use the information when you need to motivate this person again. Over a period of time, these actions and reactions will develop into a track record. By using this record, you can establish a basis from which to motivate this person in the future.

For each of the three elements we have just considered, a list of questions has been provided on pages 106 through 110. Now that you understand *2 Minute Motivation,* it is time to put it to work!

The *2 Minute Motivator* remembers that:

1. Inspiring motivation is both an opportunity and a risk.

2. Many attempts at motivation do not require significant changes in behavior.

3. Understanding the person's feelings about change is a key factor to predicting your success in motivating them.

4. A person's perception of what others will think is a crucial element in motivation.

5. Impacting a person's values will sometimes override resistance to change and what others think.

6. Effective motivation requires consistent follow-up and encouragement.

Employee's Orientation Toward Change

✓ How flexible is this employee?

✓ How open to suggestions is this person?

✓ How does he or she approach new opportunities?

✓ Describe the support this employee needs in order to make a substantial change (in position duties, work setting, level of responsibilities, etc.).

✓ How does he or she generally perceive change in the organization?

✓ When this employee is uncomfortable with a change, how does he or she react?

✓ In what cases have you observed this person welcoming change?

✓ How does he or she view change outside of work?

Employee's Perception of What Other People Think

✓ How does this employee think the organization's management feels about employee motivation?

✓ How subject is this person to peer pressure?

✓ What in the organization's culture blocks attempts at motivation?

✓ Where does this person fit into the natural leadership of the organization? (Leader or follower? Under whose influence?)

✓ What attitudes does the organization's culture have about employee motivation?

✓ Which of these attitudes help and what can be done to encourage them?

✓ Which of these attitudes hinder and what can be done to discourage them?

How the Motivational Strategy Impacts the Employee's Values

✓ How does the strategy address this employee's values and background?

✓ How effective is the strategy for this employee, based on what you have learned about him or her?

✓ What do you expect from your employee as a result of using this strategy?

Putting 2 Minute Motivation to Work

Chapter 5

Let's review what we've learned so far...

2 Minute Motivation is based on three elements:

➡ The attitudes and values of the person you are trying to motivate.

➡ Your own attitudes and values.

and

➡ The person's reaction to your attempts to motivate him or her.

We know that every person's motivation in the workplace depends on five factors, including:

➡ Job content

➡ Personal values and experiences

➠ Physical environment
➠ Perceptions of coworkers
and
➠ Observations about the person
motivating him or her

We also know that your actions as a motivator depend on six factors including your:

➠ Understanding the person's job content
➠ Observations about him or her
➠ Personal values and experiences
➠ Physical environment
➠ Perceptions of coworkers
and
➠ Results of your past efforts to motivate.

Finally, we know that your employees' reactions to motivation depend on three factors including:

➠ His or her orientation toward change
➠ Perceptions of what others will think
and
➠ The impact your attempt to motivate
has on his or her values

But how can you put this process to work on a day-to-day basis?

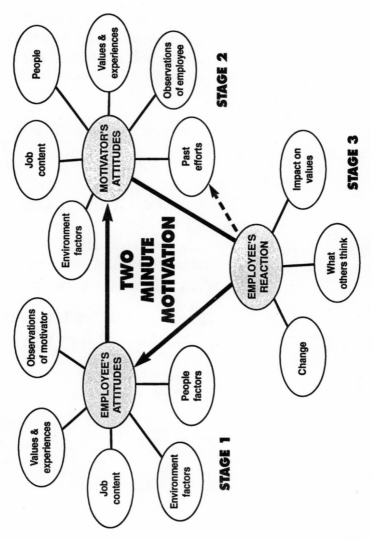

Motivation is not just talk. It is also action... and modeling. It is setting an example for others to see. Your level of enthusiasm and motivation has a direct impact on the motivation, enthusiasm and vigor of others.

In attempting to motivate someone, ask yourself three questions:

1. What are my values? What do I want to get out of this for myself? What do I want to see accomplished?
2. What are the other person's values?
3. How can I combine my values with my employee's values to better motivate them?

The phrase "walking your talk" holds true in the motivation of others more than anywhere else.

Your day-to-day tasks revolve around a series of situations. You can anticipate how someone will react to your attempts to motivate him or her by developing a better understanding of how the person thinks. Even the way the day starts may be greatly influenced by the way your employees enter the workplace. If they come in anticipating a problem with you, they will already be on their guard.

Think about the atmosphere in the office as weather. How would you describe it? Is it cloudy? Partly sunny? Stormy? You might ask others how they feel about the atmosphere in the office. While some may be reluctant to reveal their true feelings, over a period of time they may express emotions or make suggestions that provide keys to creating a more motivational atmosphere.

Sometimes it's the little comments overheard at the coffee machine which can reveal the most about what people are thinking about their jobs.

Increase your awareness about the present work environment and how people are feeling every day. You can accomplish this not only by asking them, but more importantly by observing what they say and their nonverbals and behaviors.

Keeping track of this information and reviewing it when you are looking for opportunities to motivate someone is an organized way to help you inspire that person.

You can gather this information in a number of settings. Consider the following:

General office environment: What does the employee say to others while working? How does he react to the comments of others? What makes him bristle? What does he find amusing? What off-hand comments does he make which may lead you to detect his underlying values? Is he a loner or does he often seek social contact with others?

Work habits: How well does she concentrate? Does she get the job done on time? Does she meet your expectations? How much training time or verbal direction does she need? How many questions does she ask? Is she willing to take risks to get the job done? Is she enthusiastic about the skills and abilities she is using?

Meetings: Does he participate? How does he participate? Is he a leader? Does he speak first or last? Does he have a reputation for a particular type of behavior in meetings such as making funny or caustic comments? Does he look to others for leadership? Is he independent in his way of thinking?

Social gatherings: Does he participate? How does he participate? Is he a natural leader? What is the nature of his comments? Does he have fun? How does he appear to feel about others? Are there subjects he tends to avoid? Are there subjects which dominate his conversations?

One-on-one conversations: Does she appear intimidated by you as a manager? Is she concerned about your perception of her performance? Is she comfortable in your presence? Does she feel free to make comments and contributions for the "cause"? Does she bristle at particular references especially those referring to her abilities, skills, education, age, culture and ethnicity, etc.?

In all of these job-related settings, it is wise to observe more than just the spoken word. Look for changes in voice inflection, manner of speaking, posture, eye contact, facial expressions, appearance, and level of confidence.

As you observe people, take a few seconds to assess the environment. Ask open-ended questions and investigate. Are they anticipating your moves? Do they share your enthusiasm?

If you choose to delegate a project, make sure the individual is interested in doing it. If not, ask why and then try to sell the benefits. Simply delegating something because you are in charge will not result in the best outcome. Ask about his or her concerns. The person may fear he or she cannot handle the project, and for that reason, may resist it.

Can the project be modified to fit the person's values? Can certain tasks be assigned to someone else who is stronger in that area? While this takes more effort on your part, the resulting enthusiasm is more than worth the result.

Ask.

Listen.

Learn.

Finally, give your employees enough information to make good decisions. Knowledge is power and withholding knowledge from others discourages them from attacking their jobs with vigor.

These techniques do not have to be confined to a place of business. Some of the finest areas to help others develop are through professional associations, places of worship, social clubs, and other volunteer organizations. As a volunteer leader in these places, you might consider polishing some of your motivational skills before you use them on the job. Encourage others to do the same.

Too often, we engage in the art of competitive listening, where we inflict our values on others by interrupting them. By not being able to fully express their thoughts, people may feel a sense of frustration and impatience. Being listened to is one of the most powerful motivators around.

However, we tend to anticipate and finish other people's sentences for them. The temptation of course, is to hear only what we choose to hear instead of listening to the person's entire message.

Listen, listen, listen, and you will learn, learn, learn. Use silence as an opportunity to get individuals to reveal more about themselves. Since most people find silence uncomfortable, waiting an extra second before you speak again may elicit another comment from them. You'll gain more insight into what the person is thinking.

A key to implementing any motivational strategy is to find out what the the person needs and to respond to that desire. Motivators also need to be willing to take chances. Just as a good manager takes chances in order to accomplish a particular task, a good motivator must be willing to take some chances to discover what really makes a person value his or her work.

The key to motivating an employee is to find a match between your motivational strategy and that person's values. You must overcome any obstacles to his or her motivation. These include repeated interruptions, noise distractions, physical obstacles in the working environment, and office politics, among others.

You must maintain your focus when trying to motivate that particular individual. While you may supervise a number of people, your strategies for each one must be tailored to each person's needs and values.

The support you give must be unconditional based on what your people need, not on what you want them to need. And the better you know your employees, the easier it will be to create ways to provide two-minute opportunities for motivation.

Motivation does not mean creating cash incentives (though money can help motivate people). In this case, it means giving people the opportunity to express themselves and to feel a sense of accomplishment, contribution, and value.

Following through and being consistent when motivating people is paramount for inspiring them. You must be willing to do what you say you'll do. Once you have committed to a particular motivational strategy, make sure you complete it. Do not change your plan midway through. If you do, you will only reverse any positive effects you began and, in essence, de-motivate your people.

Listen, listen, listen

and you will

learn, learn, learn.

Setting goals is a good example of this. On a periodic basis, most employees set goals when their supervisor asks them to. Yet many supervisors fail to extend continued support to their employees as they attempt to accomplish their goals. Your ability to follow through to assist your people in achieving their goals can be one of the most important steps in beginning to better motivate them.

Meet each person on your staff where that person is in his or her development on the job. In many cases, a lack of self-esteem is a major obstacle to motivation. Your ability to help your people understand that they are okay as they are now, but that they can grow to be more valuable and contribute and accomplish more in the future is essential.

As you begin to implement a motivational strategy for each individual, ask yourself a set of filter questions to help you determine whether your strategy will be effective:

1. Is this strategy serving me or serving them?
2. Does this plan keep their overall values in mind?

3. Will my people understand the purpose of my strategy?
4. Is my plan consistent with other efforts I have made to motivate my employees?

By asking yourself these four questions, you'll discover whether your plan will be effective for the individual you designed it for.

Recognize the subtle ways in which motivation takes place. You may, for instance, encourage someone to take on a particular project because you feel it would be good for his or her career. And out of respect for you, or because he or she reports to you, that person may go out and complete the project, even though he or she has no interest in it.

That person might say "yes" to you and "no" to themselves. As a result, you might react with frustration when your employee responds with less enthusiasm than you would expect. Having a clearer picture of the person's values, desires, and goals based on the two-minute opportunities you use to observe the person will help you tremendously.

Comments such as "Thank God, it's Friday," or "I'm glad it's 'hump day,'" are telling signs that someone is not enjoying the work as much as he or she could. People who arrive early and leave late may be conscientious about their position. Or they may be feeling overwhelmed. Don't assume which one it is. Instead, ask. Observe. And respond. It is your job as motivator to discover how you can best help this individual.

In addition to the immediate pat on the back and words of support you give them, you should also create a list for each individual of the other creative techniques you can use to motivate him or her. Remember that motivation takes place in two- to three-minute opportunities. Therefore, your ability to respond quickly to something a person has done is crucial.

While pats on the back and words of encouragement during staff meetings are important, they don't come close to the consistent encouragement and cheerleading that people must have on a regular basis.

Develop a file of ideas as you come across them in your reading and interactions with others. What can you use to better work with those you supervise?

Once again, as you prepare to use each one of your ideas, run them through the four-question filter we have already discussed. Be willing to take a chance with some unusual or offbeat ideas that will capture your people's attention and demonstrate that you are in touch with their values.

Fill your head with these two-minute options. Create a mental file that you can use immediately. If you wait twenty-four hours before you pat someone on the back, it is often too late to do the most good.

Your ability to discover what a person is really thinking is the key to understanding how to adjust your motivational style to fit that person's needs.

Continually seek and evaluate the formal and informal feedback you receive from your employees. What are they thinking? Do they like what you are doing? Taking two-minute opportunities to better understand your people and their values gives you essential information about what motivates them.

You cannot be too predictable, however. Using the same motivational strategy over and over will encourage cynicism. Consistency plus creativity, if nothing else, demonstrates your trust and your belief in each individual. Actions always speak louder than words.

Finally, seize the moment. Don't miss your opportunities to motivate people by putting them off until tomorrow. Don't let distractions get to you. Become more aware of the two-minute chances you have each day to motivate your people. When you develop this into a regular pattern of behavior, you'll be amazed at how productive your people will become.

The *2 Minute Motivator* remembers that:

1. You anticipate the reactions of others by understanding how they are motivated.

2. Little comments can be the most revealing about how a person thinks.

3. When you observe people, you should also evaluate the surrounding environment.

4. If you listen, listen, listen, you will learn, learn, learn!

5. Motivation is giving every person an opportunity to express him or herself and feel a sense of accomplishment.

6. Consistency and the ability to follow through are paramount for effective motivation.

7. Seizing the moment to provide encouragement will always be the best way to motivate.

Seize

the

moment

to

motivate!

Acknowledgements

So many people have contributed to this book through their ideas, support, love, and good humor—but special appreciation goes to:

Okie Arnot, Geri Bell, Troy Campbell, Brian Legget, Hillard Rest, Marty Tarabar, and Glen Yandell for their review of the content.

Gene Drumm for helping me to hammer out the model of *2 Minute Motivation*.

My many colleagues and clients who have provided two-minute motivations for me on a constant basis!

And Wendy Elliott Wendover, my own two-minute motivator!

Robert W. Wendover
Englewood, Colorado

Books by Robert Wendover...

High Performance Hiring

Smart Hiring for Your Business

2 Minute Motivation

About the Author

Robert W. Wendover is the president of Leadership Resources, Inc., a producer of publications and seminars for business. Over the past ten years, he has presented customized training and keynotes for industry, education, and government. He specializes in assisting organizations with the recruitment and motivation of employees.

Drawing information from constant research and hands-on experience in fields ranging from corporate business to education, government, hospitality, and career counseling, Bob always brings fresh perspectives on finding and keeping the top performers. His many, multi-faceted experiences help him identify with supervisors facing current management challenges, and his ongoing contact with hundreds of employers keeps him updated on the latest trends and developments in human resource management.

As an author and researcher, Bob writes more than a dozen articles per year for national and local publications such as *The Wall Street Journal's National Business Employment Weekly, Engineering Horizons, Information Management, Supervisory Management, Human Resources Professional,* and

The American Management Association's President's Letter. He is also a contributor to the *Manager's Edge* audio cassette series heard monthly by over 14,000 managers.

Bob is a former president of the Rocky Mountain Chapter of the American Society for Training and Development and past president of the Colorado Speakers Association. He has served on the faculties of the University of Denver, the University of Phoenix, and as an instructor for the University of Colorado. Along with a degree in Industrial Arts, Bob also holds degrees in Psychology and Education.

Bob's fast-paced, entertaining style makes him the perfect speaker for motivating employees or providing a thought-provoking program to kick off a conference. Here is how one participant put it: "Amid the laughter and stories was a wealth of useful information. You kept us focused and entertained at the same time." If you would like Bob to speak at your next conference, contact him at:

Leadership Resources, Inc.
7500 E. Arapahoe Road
Suite 295
Englewood, CO 80112
(800) 227-5510

2 Minute Motivation

Grow Your Business With These Small Business Books From Sourcebooks—

Smart Hiring For Your Business by Robert W. Wendover
Everything you need to know to find and hire the best employees.
  200 pages, ISBN 0-942061-57-8 (hardcover) • ISBN 0-942061-56-X (paperback)

The Small Business Start-Up Guide by Hal Root and Steve Koenig
Make or break factors to successfully launch your own business.
  152 pages, ISBN 0-942061-70-5 (hardcover) • ISBN 0-942061-67-5 (paperback)

Getting Paid In Full by W. Kelsea Wilber (August 1994)
Collect the money you are owed and develop a successful credit policy.
  144 pages, ISBN 0-942061-71-3 (hardcover) • ISBN 0-942061-68-3 (paperback)

How To Sharpen Your Competitive Edge by Don Reynolds, Jr.
Finding, developing and capitalizing on crackerjack positioning!
  200 pages, ISBN 0-942061-73-X (hardcover) • ISBN 0-942061-72-1 (paperback)

Protect Your Business by Sgt. James Nelson and Ofc.Terry Davis (August 1994)
Top cops help you safeguard your business against shoplifting, employee theft, and more.
  144 pages, ISBN 0-942061-69-1 (hardcover) • ISBN 0-942061-66-7 (paperback

How to Market Your Business by Ian B. Rosengarten, MS, MPH
An introduction to the tools and tactics for marketing your business.
  152 pages, ISBN 0-942061-48-9 (hardcover) • ISBN 0-942061-45-4 (paperback)

How to Get a Loan or Line of Credit for Your Business by Bryan E. Milling
A banker show you exactly what you need to do to get a loan.
  152 pages, ISBN 0-942061-46-2 (hardcover) • ISBN 0-942061-43-8 (paperback)

Your First Business Plan by Joseph Covello and Brian Hazelgren
Learn the critical steps to writing a business plan.
  152 pages, ISBN 0-942061-47-0 (hardcover) • ISBN 0-942061-44-6 (paperback)

The Small Business Survival Guide by Robert E. Fleury
Learn to manage your cash, profits and taxes. Plus, **No Entry Accounting**—an easy way of doing and understanding your own accounting without double entry bookkeeping.
256 pages, ISBN 0-942061-11-X (hardcover) $29.95 • ISBN 0-942061-12-8 (paperback) **$17.95**

Small Claims Court Without A Lawyer by W. Kelsea Wilber, Attorney-at-Law
File a claim and get a judgment quickly and economically. Written in clear, uncomplicated language, it includes details about each state's small claims court system.
  224 pages, ISBN 0-942061-32-2 (paperback) **$18.95**

To order these books or any other of our many publications, please contact your local bookseller or call Sourcebooks at 1-800-798-2475. Get a copy of our catalog by writing or faxing:

Sourcebooks, Inc.
P. O. Box 372
Naperville, IL 60566
(708) 961-3900
FAX: (708) 961-2168

Thank you for your interest!

Would You Like to Be In Our Next Book?

We're compiling a series of books that feature the best small business ideas. These can be ideas to save money, make money, motivate employees, increase sales, market your service, take care of your equipment needs, finance your business, collect money from creditors, negotiate a lease, improve customer service, develop team management, recruit new employees, develop new products, manage your sales force…in short, *ideas that really made a difference to the way you successfully run your business.* **We'd love to include your ideas!** We will, of course, give you credit for any ideas we publish. *Submissions become the property of the publisher.*

Please send your suggestions on your letterhead to:

Attn: "New Ideas" Dept.
Small Business Sourcebooks Series
P.O. Box 372
Naperville, IL 60566

Please be sure to include your name, address, phone number, FAX number if you have one and any pertinent information about your business (for example, a description of your business, the number of employees, your position). And again,
Thank You for working with Sourcebooks.

A Note from the Publisher

Hello!

I'm Dominique Raccah, head of Sourcebooks, Inc. In our business book series we've tried to bring you easy-to-use material to help you improve your key business skills. We've developed this series, with the help of a lot of entrepreneurs like yourself, to tackle some of the more common problems in building a business. As updated editions of these books are published, your input will be invaluable.

Please take the time to jot down any ideas you may have about the books you are using:

- Was the book useful?
- What would you like more of? What would you like less of?
- What else should be in this series?
- What are the most difficult areas facing you as you grow your business?

Please make sure you tell us which book you were using at the time. And please include your name, address and phone number so we can let you know if we incorporate your suggestions.

Thank You For Your Time and Your Support.

With Best Regards,

Dominique Raccah
and the staff of

Sourcebooks, Inc.
Small Business Sourcebooks
P.O. Box 372
Naperville, IL 60566
(708) 961-3900   FAX: (708) 961-2168

Do You Service Small Business Clients Too?

We, at Sourcebooks, have developed our business book program to serve the needs of the small business community. We've gotten incredible response to this series. If you are an accountant, lawyer, banker or consultant who also serves the small business community and you think our books could be of use to your clients, please give us a call. We offer special discounts to people who purchase these books to give or sell to their clients. Please contact us at 708-961-3900 or write to us at the address listed above for details. We'd love to work with you